The Fruit of the Spirit

Cultivating Christlike Character

STUART BRISCOE

FISHERMAN
BIBLE STUDY SERIES

THE FRUIT OF THE SPIRIT
PUBLISHED BY WATERBROOK PRESS
12265 Oracle Blvd., Suite 200
Colorado Springs, Colorado 80921

Trade Paperback ISBN 978-0-87788-258-9

Published in the United States by WaterBrook Multnomah, an imprint of the
Crown Publishing Group, a division of Penguin Random House LLC, New York.

Printed in the United States of America

2016

Contents

How to Use This Studyguide

F isherman studyguides are based on the inductive approach to Bible study. Inductive study is discovery study; we discover what the Bible says as we ask questions about its content and search for answers. This is quite different from the process in which a teacher *tells* a group *about* the Bible—what it means and what to do about it. In inductive study, God speaks directly to each of us through his Word.

A group functions best when a leader keeps the discussion on target, but the leader is neither the teacher nor the "answer person." A leader's responsibility is to *ask*—not *tell*. The answers come from the text itself as group members examine, discuss, and think together about the passage.

There are four kinds of questions in each study. The first is an *approach question*. Asked and answered before the Bible passage is read, this question breaks the ice and helps you start thinking about the topic of the Bible study. It begins to reveal where thoughts and feelings need to be transformed by Scripture.

Some of the earlier questions in each study are *observation questions*—who, what, where, when, and how—designed to help you learn some basic facts about the passage of Scripture.

Once you know what the Bible says, you need to ask, *What does it mean?* These *interpretation questions* help you discover the writer's basic message.

Next come *application questions,* which ask, *What does it mean to me?* They challenge you to live out the Scripture's life-transforming message.

Fisherman studyguides provide spaces between questions for jotting down responses as well as any related questions you would like to raise in the group. Each group member should have a copy of the studyguide and may take a turn in leading the group.

A group should use any accurate, modern translation of the Bible such as the *New International Version,* the *New American Standard Bible,* the *New Living Translation,* the *New Revised Standard Version,* the *New Jerusalem Bible,* or the *Good News Bible.* (Other translations or paraphrases of the Bible may be referred to when additional help is needed.) Bible commentaries should not be brought to a Bible study because they tend to dampen discussion and keep people from thinking for themselves.

Suggestions for Group Leaders

1. Thoroughly read and study the Bible passage before the meeting. Get a firm grasp on its themes and begin applying its teachings for yourself. Pray that the Holy Spirit will "guide you into all truth" (John 16:13) so that your leadership will guide others.

2. If any of the studyguide's questions seem ambiguous or unnatural to you, rephrase them, feeling free to add others that seem necessary to bring out the meaning of a verse.

3. Begin (and end) the study promptly. Start by asking someone to pray that every participant will both understand the passage and be open to its transforming power. Remember, the Holy Spirit is the teacher, not you!

4. Ask for volunteers to read the passages aloud.

5. As you ask the studyguide's questions in sequence, encourage everyone to participate in the discussion. If some are silent, try gently suggesting, "Let's have an answer from someone who hasn't spoken up yet."

6. If a question comes up that you can't answer, don't be afraid to admit that you're baffled. Assign the topic as a research project for someone to report on next week, or say, "I'll do some studying and let you know what I find out."

7. Keep the discussion moving, but be sure it stays focused. Though a certain number of tangents are inevitable, you'll want to quickly bring the discussion back to the topic at hand. Also, learn to pace the discussion so that you finish the lesson in the time allotted.

8. Don't be afraid of silences; some questions take time to answer, and some people need time to gather courage to speak. If silence persists, rephrase your question, but resist the temptation to answer it yourself.

9. If someone comes up with an answer that is clearly illogical or unbiblical, ask for further clarification: "What verse suggests that to you?"

10. Discourage overuse of cross references. Learn all you can from the passage at hand, while selectively incorporating a few important references suggested in the studyguide.

11. Some questions are marked with a ✐. This indicates that further information is available in the Leader's Notes at the back of the guide.

12. For more information on getting a new Bible study group started and keeping it functioning effectively, read *You Can Start a Bible Study Group* by Gladys M. Hunt and *Pilgrims in Progress: Growing Through Groups* by Jim and Carol Plueddemann. (Both books are available from Shaw Books.)

Suggestions for Group Members

1. Learn and apply the following ground rules for effective Bible study. (If new members join the group later, review these guidelines with the whole group.)

2. Remember that your goal is to learn all you can *from the Bible passage being studied.* Let it speak for itself without using Bible commentaries or other Bible passages. There is more than enough in each assigned passage to keep your group productively occupied for one session. Sticking to the passage saves the group from insecurity ("I don't have the right reference books—or the time to read anything else.") and confusion ("Where did *that* come from? I thought we were studying _____.").

3. Avoid the temptation to bring up those fascinating tangents that don't really grow out of the passage you are discussing. If the topic is of common interest, you can bring it up later in informal conversation after the study. Meanwhile, help one another stick to the subject.

4. Encourage one another to participate. People remember best what they discover and verbalize for

themselves. Some people are naturally shy, while others may be afraid of making a mistake. If your discussion is free and friendly and you show real interest in what other group members think and feel, the quieter ones will be more likely to speak up. Remember, the more people involved in a discussion, the richer it will be.

5. Guard yourself from answering too many questions or talking too much. Give others a chance to share their ideas. If you are one who participates easily, discipline yourself by counting to ten before you open your mouth.

6. Make personal, honest applications and commit yourself to letting God's Word change you.

Introduction

On rare occasions I go grocery shopping with my wife, and I love to see the variety of colors and shapes and smells in the produce section. I watch customers pick up the plums and squeeze them. They lift grapes up to the light, polish apples, inspect oranges, look at the bottom of the little green baskets of strawberries. Then they make their choices.

It is not uncommon for Christians to treat the fruit of the Spirit in the same way. Some people are very loving and squeeze love for all they can get out of it. Others are joyful to a fault and spend much time polishing their jokes and their teeth. Faithful people take everything seriously and carefully hold their motives up to the light, and the self-controlled peer under the baskets of their actions, looking carefully for any signs of overripeness.

But like buyers in a fruit store, they sometimes concentrate on the fruit that interests them or comes easily to them, without bothering with other aspects of the fruit of the Spirit. Sometimes the really loving person is not self-controlled, and frequently the joyful one is not at all gentle. It's hard for gentle people to be faithful when faithfulness requires drastic action, while occasionally the faithful have been known to exercise their faithfulness with such enthusiasm that their kindness has been open to question.

In these studies we will learn that when it comes to living by the Spirit, we do not have the freedom to pick and choose what fruit we do or do not want to exhibit. All of the fruit of the Spirit is to be desired and cultivated in our lives as we abide in Christ. We will also see that, realistically, under some circumstances one aspect of the fruit may be more appropriate than another, without in any way suggesting that it is more important than another.

James explored the link between behavior and belief in his epistle, under the headings of "faith" and "works." He insisted that faith without works is dead, reminding us not only that belief behaves but that correct belief behaves properly. The Lord Jesus made a similar point when he explained that people could be known by their fruit in much the same way that trees and plants can be identified by their produce.

It's one thing to believe that Christ died for the sins of the world—no doubt this belief affects behavior. But it is entirely different to believe that Christ died for *me* and then rose again to live within me through the Holy Spirit. To believe this is to be introduced to vast possibilities of unique behavior.

The fruit of the Spirit is most definitely the result of inner workings of the blessed Holy Spirit, without which no such thing as Spirit life would be possible. But there is also a human factor. The Spirit life is a product of both Spirit activity and human response. It comes from *obedience* to God's commands to love, be patient, kind, and self-controlled, but it also requires *dependence* on God's power, through the Spirit, to make it possible.

So come learn for the first time, or in a deeper way, how your believing can affect your behaving. May this study of the fruit of the Spirit renew and refresh you, and enable you to abide more in Jesus, our source of life.

Spirit Life: "Let Us Keep in Step with the Spirit"

GALATIANS 5:16-26; JOHN 15:1-8

Just for fun I once asked two friends, "How many fruits of the Spirit are there?" One said eight and the other replied nine. "You're both wrong," I countered. "It says 'the *fruit* of the Spirit *is*,' not the '*fruits* of the Spirit *are*.'" This may seem like hairsplitting, but it is significant.

If we think of *fruit* rather than *fruits*, we take away the freedom to be picky about the fruit we like and the behavior we choose. The fruit of the Spirit is to be seen not as a collection of unrelated fruits that can be selected according to personal preference, but rather as a composite description of our lives. Our all-around behavior is the direct result of a relationship with the living Lord who indwells his people by his Spirit.

1. Give an example of how your beliefs affected your behavior in a specific way today.

READ GALATIANS 5:16-26.

2. What conflict is described in verses 16-18?

In what ways have you experienced this struggle in your own life?

3. What are the results of living by the Spirit (verses 16,18,22,23)?

4. How might living by the Spirit affect the actions and attitudes Paul listed in verses 19-21?

↗ 5. How do you reconcile Paul's warning in verse 21 with his statement in verse 26, which shows that those in the kingdom also struggle with these sins?

↗ 6. Contrast *crucifying* the sinful nature with *living* by the Spirit. How are these two aspects of the Spirit life related?

7. What do you think is involved in keeping "in step with the Spirit" (verse 25)? How do we do this?

READ JOHN 15:1-8.

8. Who is the vine and the gardener, and who are the branches?

   Why is this metaphor a good one for the truth Jesus was teaching?

9. What is significant about the reciprocal relationship emphasized in this passage (verses 4,5,7)?

10. How does Christ remain in us?

    Name some ways we can remain in him.

11. What are some of the results of remaining in Jesus (verses 7-8)?

What might result if we fail to remain in him?

12. In what respect is a Christian responsible for the growth of fruit in his or her life?

13. What is the role of the Holy Spirit in this growth?

Love: "Love Each Other as I Have Loved You"

JOHN 15:9-17; MARK 12:28-34

Love is...a warm puppy...never having to say you're sorry...like the measles—everybody catches it some-time. Love has inspired some to die and others to kill. It may make the world go 'round, but it certainly causes a lot of con-fusion in the process.

This confusion has found its way into spiritual experience because of the high priority given to love in biblical revelation. "God is love," we are told, and we are commanded to love. It heads the list of the fruit of the Spirit as well as being one of the things that will remain forever. What then is this love of which Christians speak so often and sing so loudly?

1. In what ways has love's meaning been confused in your own life?

- Sex
- To be used to gain advantage
- "Well if you Loved me..."
- It's just another 4-letter word
- Love should be shown/not said

READ JOHN 15:9-17.

2. What is involved in *remaining* in Jesus' love?

- Sacrafice
- other's First

3. What is love as Jesus defined it?

Everlasting

4. Give some examples of how God has modeled his love for us.

-Created Earth to Rid Heaven of Evil so we may live in a Forever paradise

5. What is significant about being Jesus' *friends* rather than his servants?

-Shows we know how to Love

6. What does it mean to you that Jesus has chosen and appointed you to bear fruit?

    - tough one, why then is it so hard for me to love?

7. How can we emulate Jesus' love and fulfill his command in verse 17?

    Love eachother

READ MARK 12:28-34.

8. How is the definition of love expanded here?

    - Agape love
    - First we must love God & Then the rest comes?

9. Restate verse 30 in your own words.

    - Love must consume us!

10. What does it mean to love your neighbor *as yourself?*

    - They need help, help them
    - Do to them as you would want done
    - Q: Christian or un-christian neighbors = ?

11.   What added insight in the teacher's answer made Jesus affirm him as he did in verse 34?

    - He is Fullfilling
    Gods Fullness

12.   Consider the relationship between love for God, love for self, and love for one's neighbor. How are these bound together in the Spirit life?

    - Thoughts become Actions
    - What's in a man's heart
    * he is!*

13.   What one step can you take this week to respond to the challenge of meeting a hurting world with God's love?

    - That's hard for me!
    * Pray for me!*

Joy: "In Him Our Hearts Rejoice"

PSALM 33:1-11,20-22; 1 PETER 1:3-9

Really?

C hristians often have the reputation of being very serious people, even to the point of gloominess. We speak of sin and judgment, the cross and shed blood. Our awe of God and solemnity in light of the human condition are appropriate. Nevertheless, our lives are supposed to be characterized by joy. ← *But How?*

That God approves of his people's being joyful is thoroughly attested to in Scripture. The Israelites came before God with joy in religious festivals. David danced with joy before the Lord. The angels proclaimed a message of "great joy" as they announced Jesus' birth. Jesus lived a life "full of joy through the Holy Spirit" (Luke 10:21). God has given us beauty in nature and love in relationships to stimulate our joy as they mirror for us the invisible attributes of God. And even in suffering we can learn to rejoice in God's grace and presence and in what he will accomplish through it. *Need Balance!*

Bible also shows 50/50 of the mentioned people

1. In what kinds of experiences have you found real joy?

   -Kids
   -Defense (teaching).
   - Peoples dreams come true

READ PSALM 33:1-11,20-22.

2. Who is to sing to the Lord in praise?

   US

3. How are praise and joy related?

   Showing us being Thankful

4. Do you think it is *always* fitting to praise God? Why?

5. The psalmist described several ways of expressing joy in verses 1-3 and 20-21. How do you express joy in your relationship with God?

- Not often enough

- Haven't felt joy in the Lord in a very long time

6. Verses 6 and 7 show God as Creator. Give some examples of how God can use creation to stimulate joy in the believer.

- I smile + feel peaceful in His creation

7. What connection does hope have to joy (verses 20-22)?

- something to look forward too!

8. What trustworthy aspects of God's character do you note from this psalm?

- Now steps creating or we are seeing the Future unfold as He desired it

How does this knowledge affect your joy as a Christian?

- Not much !

READ 1 PETER 1:3-9.

9. What does our new birth in Christ give us (verses 3-5)?

A hope + future

10. Why could these first-century Christians have joy despite persecution?

11. Why does God sometimes allow Christians to suffer (verses 7-9)?

Maybe Where I have been?

12. How can Christians retain a joyful faith in difficult times?

-Grace + Future paradise

What might this kind of joy in the midst of suffering look and feel like?

- Persaverance + me!

13. How does your faith compare with the descriptions in this passage and in Psalm 33?

.vs 13-17

Take some time to pray, asking God to help you grow in a joyful faith.

-yes!
- My Hardest Fruit?
"Joy"

Peace: "The Peace of God...Will Guard Your Hearts"

ROMANS 5:1-8; 12:16-21; PHILIPPIANS 4:4-9

We usually define *peace* in negative terms such as the "absence of tension" or "living without hostility." When we regard peace only as the absence of conflict or tension, we may feel that the way to peace is in manipulating our circumstances to eliminate stress.

Augustine of Hippo captured a more biblical view in his definition of *peace* as "the tranquility of order." For the Christian, there are three applications of the experience of peace. We have "peace with God," or spiritual order; "peace on earth," or relational order; and "the peace of God," or psychological order. True peace is that overall sense of well-being that comes from knowing that, our lives are in God's control.

1. When was the last time you felt "at peace"? What made you feel that way?

READ ROMANS 5:1-8.

Peace with God: Spiritual Order

2. According to this passage, what does it mean to have peace with God (see also 5:10)?

3. In what things can we rejoice (verses 2-3)?

How would these things contribute to our peace?

4. What is the Holy Spirit's part in securing our hope (verse 5)? What do you think is our part?

5. How does God's demonstration of love in Christ affect your overall peace of mind?

READ ROMANS 12:16-21.

Peace on Earth: Relational Order

6. What things prevent us from living in harmony with others?

7. Why not repay evil with evil?

✒ 8. What actions will result from taking seriously Paul's command in verse 18?

How do you live this out when the other party doesn't cooperate?

9. What is difficult about following the principle in verse 20?

Have you ever been treated like this by someone else? How did you respond?

10. How does having peace with God affect your ability to live peacefully with others?

Read Philippians 4:4-9.

The Peace of God: Psychological Order

⌖ 11. What is Paul's prescription for having the peace of God?

How does this differ from our culture's view of achieving inner peace?

12. What is the relationship between prayer and the peace of God?

✎ 13.   Paul encourages us not to be anxious about any-
        thing. Is all anxiety sin, or are there times when
        anxiety and concern are appropriate? Discuss.

✎ 14.   How does having peace *with* God affect your ability
        to experience the peace *of* God?

Patience: "Bear with Each Other"

MATTHEW 18:21-35; COLOSSIANS 3:12-14

L ife cannot be lived in isolation. We live in the context of relationships, good or bad. Impatience and anger, justifiable or not, are often our responses to unpleasant situations and people.

Just as God models for us love, joy, and peace, we see that he is also the perfect example of patience in relationships. His wrath and anger against sin are quite real. But this righteous anger is "slowed down" by his great love for us. He is longsuffering and patient with us, and asks us to be the same with others. With so many frustrating situations in our lives, we have boundless opportunity for the fruit of the Spirit to blossom into patience.

1. When do you get most impatient: with irritating people or irritating circumstances? Explain.

READ MATTHEW 18:21-35.

2. What did the first servant ask of his master? Why do you think he then responded to his fellow servant so differently?

3. Half of the Greek word for *patience* in verse 26 *(makrothumia)* means "anger" and the other half means "long" or "slow" (i.e., handling anger slowly). What does this definition tell us about how we are to apply patience?

4. What is the relationship between forgiveness and patience?

⤢ 5. Are you comfortable with a God who expresses both wrath and patience? Why or why not?

6. Name some ways you have seen people express impatience and anger inappropriately.

What is God's solution to this problem?

READ COLOSSIANS 3:12-14.

7. Paul described the believers in Colosse in the beginning of verse 12 as "God's chosen people, holy and dearly loved." Do you see yourself like this? Why or why not?

8. How does knowing how God sees us affect how we treat other people?

9. Paul listed several virtues that express love and patience. In what ways can this kind of loving patience benefit families, churches, and the world?

10. What theme is echoed in this passage that was also stated in the parable in Matthew 18?

11. How has God expressed his patience to you?

12. Is there someone in your life right now toward whom you need to show patience?

Kindness: "Be Kind and Compassionate to One Another"

2 SAMUEL 9; EPHESIANS 2:4-7

K indness is not looked upon favorably by everyone. There are those who feel that kindness carries a cost they are not prepared to pay. It is too time consuming, too demanding, too likely to interfere with their own plans.

Spirit life, however, insists that kindness is not an inconvenience to be avoided, but a characteristic to be embraced. After all, God has lavished his lovingkindness on us through Christ. As we study David's example of kindness, we'll see that it involves treating others with sympathy, benevolence, and generosity. All of these attitudes are essentially practical; none is less than costly.

1. What are some results of kindness that you've seen in your life or someone else's?

READ 2 SAMUEL 9.

2. Why was it important to David to show kindness to Saul's family (verse 1)? (See also 1 Samuel 20:12-17.)

3. Keeping in mind that Saul had been David's mortal enemy, what reasons would David have had for *not* doing this?

What does this action reveal about David's character?

4. Do you think David was just dutifully fulfilling his covenant with Jonathan? What evidence do you find here for your answer?

5. As Jonathan's dear friend and also as king of Israel, what mixed emotions might David have felt when he saw Jonathan's son, Mephibosheth?

6. Why would Mephibosheth have had reason to be afraid of King David?

7. What specific actions did David's kindness lead to (verse 7)?

8. How do you think David's kindness made Mephibosheth feel?

9. What overall aspects and effects of kindness can you glean from this story?

READ EPHESIANS 2:4-7.

10. How has God shown kindness to us? What is his motivation?

⌀ 11. In what ways are grace and kindness intertwined?

12. Read Ephesians 4:32 in closing. Is there a current situation in which you are struggling to be kind? What makes it hard for you to be compassionate in this situation?

Pray for a renewed understanding of God's lovingkindness to you, asking the Holy Spirit to help you show this same kindness to others.

Goodness: "The Lord Is Good"

PSALM 100, ROMANS 7:18-20; 12:9,21

G ood and *goodness* are two of our most popular words. As children we are encouraged to "be good," and as adults we like to think we are "doing good." We all know that evil is the opposite of good, and there is broad agreement that the path of goodness is the right way to go. But for a long time there has been a debate on what constitutes goodness. Is it the experience of pleasure and the eradication of pain? Is it the acquisition of knowledge? Is it doing to others what you want them to do to you? Is it the greatest good for the greatest number? Is it having lots of good things?

Before being good and doing good, we first need to define *goodness*. Any consideration of the goodness of Spirit life, while being aware of human concepts of goodness, must have a different point of reference. God, not man, is the measure of all things, including goodness.

1. Do you think you are a "good" person? Why?

READ PSALM 100.

2. What is affirmed about God's character in this psalm?

⌁ 3. How do God's actions reflect his goodness?

4. Note the psalmist's joyful response. How do you usually respond to God's goodness in your life?

⌁ 5. How does God's goodness determine the meaning of ultimate good?

READ ROMANS 7:18-20.

⌁ 6. What is affirmed about human nature in this passage?

7. What is the battleground for the fight between good and evil?

8. Can you relate to Paul's struggle? Why or why not?

   How do you handle the tension he describes?

9. How does this struggle in us affect our ability to exhibit goodness?

READ ROMANS 12:9,21.

10. What different aspects of goodness and doing good are implied in Paul's two statements?

🖋 11. What are some evils in our society?

What does it mean to *hate* them?

🖋 12. Give an example of clinging to good in the midst of evil.

🖋 13. What might be involved in overcoming evil with good?

Is this an active or passive process? In what way?

14. What part does the Holy Spirit play in developing goodness in our lives?

Faithfulness: "Well Done, Good and Faithful Servant"

LAMENTATIONS 3:19-24; MATTHEW 25:14-30

F aithfulness is an integral part of human existence, so important that without it society would disintegrate. Every morning of our lives demands an eye-opening act of faith that rushes us into a series of trusting actions and dependent attitudes. We breathe air we cannot see (most of the time), eat food we don't examine, keep appointments with people we trust to be there, and board planes we trust will stay in the air. Truly we live by faith because we were created to operate in the environment of dependence as surely as fish were made for water.

But faith requires faithfulness, or it will produce only disaster. When you trust a leading pain reliever and get cyanide, trust a banker and get a crook, trust a husband and get an alcoholic, you will understand the importance of faithfulness and the disaster of faithlessness. One of life's greatest treasures is the knowledge that with God there is no false advertising, no deceptive business practices, and no broken contracts. He is utterly faithful. Upon this we can build lives set upon a rock; without this we have only sinking sand.

    1. In general terms, how have people been unfaithful to you, and how did that make you feel?

READ LAMENTATIONS 3:19-24.

    2. Why did the writer have hope in his desperate situation?

    3. How is God's faithfulness described?

4. Name one way you have seen God's faithfulness in your life recently.

⟋ 5. What is the Christian's basis for being faithful?

READ MATTHEW 25:14-30.

6. For what were the servants rewarded? For what was the lazy servant punished?

7. What do you think was Jesus' main point in this parable?

8. Why is faithfulness an important part of Spirit life?

9. What does this story add to your understanding of what it means to be faithful?

10. What "talents" has God given you?

11. How can you be faithful in using these gifts for his glory?

Meekness: "I Am Gentle and Humble in Heart"

NUMBERS 12:1-15; MATTHEW 11:28-30

R obert Ringer wrote a book called *Looking Out for No. 1,* which became a best seller. This was a surprise to me because most people I have met could probably have written it and hardly needed to read it. Against our culture's emphasis on being aggressive, standing up for your rights, and speaking out, Jesus' teaching that "the meek shall inherit the earth" looks impractical and naive.

The word *meekness* suffers because it rhymes with *weakness,* and the two have become synonymous in people's minds. We'll see from Moses' and Jesus' lives that being meek is not being weak, and it doesn't usually come naturally. Like every other aspect of Spirit life, meekness—also called gentleness— is possible through obedience to and dependence upon the Spirit of Christ, who himself was gentle and humble in heart.

1. What's the difference between meekness and weakness?

   Meakness is how you conduct your behavior
   weakness allows others to conduct it For you.

READ NUMBERS 12:1-15.

2. Why were Miriam and Aaron upset with their brother Moses?

Because whare he married

What was implied by their questions?

Dooistful - God uses us too!

3. With God's opinion of Moses stated in verses 6-9, how *could* Moses have responded to his siblings' criticism?

Rebuked them, despised them

Have you ever been in a situation like Moses where you had the upper hand? How did you respond?

A lot, Not to well.
But, I'm Learning

4. What aspects of gentleness and meekness do we see in Moses' reactions in this passage?

Asks God to Heal, Have
Mercy upon Someone
who was bitter against him

READ MATTHEW 11:28-30.

5. What does Jesus invite us to do? What does he promise?

- Co to Nhm, take his yoke
- Rest

6. What attitudes of the head and heart are involved in coming to Jesus in this way?

- Surrender
- Release Anxiety/Frustration

7. Note how Jesus described himself. What's the difference between being gentle and humble in heart and being spinelessly submissive?

- Choice .vs No choice
- Rest .vs Always Frustrated

8. How can we learn meekness from Jesus' example?

- Molding us like pottery with clay

9. Read the following verses and discuss the areas mentioned in which we are called to live with gentleness and humility.

Galatians 6:1

Help them Gently
- But watch yourself!

2 Timothy 2:24-25

I have not been
very Good with
This!

James 1:21

1 Peter 3:3-4

1 Peter 3:15

10. How do our different temperaments and personalities affect how we express this fruit of the Spirit? (In other words: Does being meek and gentle always mean being quiet and soft-spoken?)

- I Think so
- Not what we say, But How we say it!
    It's in the tone!

11. Define *meekness* in your own words.

- Relaxed, Approachable, Even tempered.

12. Is there a circumstance in your life right now in which you need to show the true strength of meekness? If you are doing this study in a group, share this if you wish and pray for one another.

- Work
- Couple Church Folk
- Family

"Im a mess!"

Self-Control: "Add to Your Faith... Self-Control"

1 CORINTHIANS 9:19-27; 2 PETER 1:3-7

Personal freedom is a wonderful aspect of living in a free society and being a child of God. But personal freedom can be like a highway with a ditch on either side. One ditch is called legalism and the other licentiousness. Legalism limits freedom with carefully defined structures and restrictions; licentiousness celebrates freedom and encourages the enjoyment of it to the point of excess, which eventually destroys the very thing it celebrates.

In a sense, self-control involves handling this freedom properly and not falling into either ditch. The Greek word for *self-control* literally means "self-mastery." Our goal should be to master those things that would mar our lives in such a way that we can be liberated to serve God and others in glorious freedom.

1. Which of the following motivations for personal
    discipline or self-control did you grow up with?
    Discuss.

    — "Remember: God sees everything."
    "What will the neighbors think?"
    "Christians don't do that."
    "Use your own judgment."
    "Anything goes!"

    *But those that told me
    this, did not have self-control.
    Was it said so they could control
    at least something? Something
    other than themselves?*

READ 1 CORINTHIANS 9:19-27.

2. What was Paul's motivation and ultimate purpose
    for limiting and adapting his own freedom?

    to relate to All men,

3. What dangers are there in being all things to all
    people?

    *- temptation
    - Loose yourself, who you are
    ~ Where do you stand, You might
      seem like a undesire person.*

How does self-control limit these dangers and free
the Christian?

odd Question!

4. Why is the analogy of an athlete a good one for the
Christian walk?

*Only one will win, compete
anyways. You'll be an winner
overcomes in your own Personal
Competition*

5. What aspects of your own Christian walk require
more self-control and discipline?

- Letting others get to me
- Less of me, more of Him
- Stop thinking, I got this.

READ 2 PETER 1:3-7.

6. What has God provided to help us live godly lives
(verses 3-4)?

Great promises
-virtue
- Knowledge
→- Self control
-Steadfastness
-Godliness
-Brotherly Affection
→- Love

7. Which of the areas in verses 5-7 are most important
    to you right now? Why?

    -Love
    -too many reasons
      It'll help me overcome
    Personall issues

8. How are self-control and perseverance related?

    -Picture an Athlote
      control ones self to persevere

9. Compare and contrast this list with the fruit of the
    Spirit in Galatians 5:22-23.

    -Interesting
    Self-control
    Love are in Both!

10. How do you balance making "every effort" with
    depending on the Holy Spirit to bring forth these
    qualities in your life?

    Check every opertunity
    -Slow down, got our
      minds off of ourselves.
    Let the spirit Lead!

11. Think back over the topics and passages we have studied. How do you now define what the fruit of the Spirit is?

Ongoing Growing process
-Different fruit have diff.
Seasons
-All Fruit with seeds reproduce

12. What in these studies has challenged you in a new way?

All of it!

Pray for renewed vigor in living the Spirit life.

Leader's Notes

STUDY 1: SPIRIT LIFE

Question 5. Paul emphasizes the fact that people who *live* like this (as a lifestyle), who continue to ignore their sin, and who refuse to change reveal that they are not born of the Spirit. The reality of a believer's new life in the Spirit is shown not by our never sinning, but by a repentant heart, open to God's Spirit.

Question 6. "In order to accept Christ as Savior, we need to turn from our sins and willingly nail our sinful nature to the cross. This doesn't mean, however, that we will never see traces of its evil desires again. As Christians we still have the capacity to sin, but we have been set free from sin's power over us and no longer have to give in to it. We must daily commit our sinful tendencies to God's control, daily crucify them, and moment by moment draw on the Spirit's power to overcome them (see Galatians 2:20 and 6:14)" (*Life Application Bible*, Wheaton, Ill.: Tyndale, 1991, p. 2126).

STUDY 2: LOVE

Question 3. Jesus defined love as selfless giving for others, and the words for love that he used enrich its meaning. In the Greek language in which the New Testament was written, three words were available to speak of love. *Eros,* from which we get the word *erotic,* has to do with the sexual, physical aspects of love, and it desires to possess for personal benefit. *Phileo,* from which we get such words as *Philadelphia* and *philanthropy,* is companionship and friendship love. (*Phileo* is used in John 15:19.) *Agape* is the word that describes God's love for us and the love that God produces and looks for in us. Agape is the fruit of a decision that commits itself to the well-being of the beloved regardless of the condition or reaction of the one loved. (*Agape* is used in John 15:9-13,17.)

Question 4. God's love for humanity was first shown in Creation, creating us and providing for us. It was seen over and over again in the long and trying relationship between Jehovah and the children of Israel in the Old Testament, waiting, persisting, forgiving. It is fully seen in the Incarnation and in Jesus' death for a lost and antagonistic world.

Question 7. Love, for many Christians and unbelievers, is more often related to "liking somebody a lot" than to choosing to be concerned for someone else's welfare. Love is a choice, and it is immensely practical. See 1 Corinthians 13:4-7 for Paul's beautiful statement of love in action.

Question 10. The idea of self-love raises a few eyebrows because we know that Christians are taught to deny themselves (see Mark 8:34-35). But we confuse *selfhood* with *selfishness.* We cannot endorse the inordinate self-love and self-gratification of our contemporary world. But that does not mean we should fail to appreciate our unique selfhood and the worth we have as God's children. It is not really possible to love others when we are filled with hatred toward ourselves.

STUDY 3: JOY

Question 5. The Hebrew of the Old Testament and the Greek of the New Testament use a number of different words to express the joy and rejoicing that are aspects of the fruit of the Spirit. The word *joyfully* in Psalm 33:1 comes from the Hebrew word *rinnah,* which literally means "to creak" and conveys the idea of exuberant expression of joy with particular reference to shouting. *Rejoice* in Psalm 33:21 comes from *simchah,* which literally means "to brighten."

Question 10. It is critical for us to understand that joy comes from rightly understanding and appreciating theological truth. To be at peace, to stand in grace is to know the exhilaration of forgiveness, acceptance, sufficiency, and assurance that our salvation brings.

Question 12. The suffering on the outside needs to be peeled away to reveal the quality of perseverance and genuineness that cannot be learned without pressure. Rather than something to be avoided, resented, or denied, the suffering allowed by a loving Father is designed to accomplish the maturing process in the believer. It is in this that we can rejoice. (See Romans 5:3-5.)

Question 13. To some, joy and trusting come easily; to others these things are a struggle. Those to whom certain aspects of the Spirit life are difficult must remember the balance between the Holy Spirit and our wills. It is in dependence upon the working of the Spirit as well as in direct obedience to the commands of Scripture that these things become real in one's life.

STUDY 4: PEACE

Question 8. Paul is wonderfully practical in Romans 12:18. The apostle does not lay on us the impossible burden of living in a state of peace with everyone in a hostile world. But he does require that we do what is necessary from our side.

Question 11. Look beyond Philippians 4:6 and use the entire passage for clues to experiencing the peace of God.

Question 13. There is a legitimate concern for others and a healthy kind of "fear" that are not necessarily sin. Paul struggled deeply and felt great concern over the newly started churches (see 2 Corinthians 11:28). If your car is swerving off the road or if you are facing an abusive situation, you need some healthy anxiety to help you fight for survival. There are also some types of emotional depression and phobias that are biologically based and can be treated medically.

But those who are habitual worriers, who live in the fog of anxiety, need to recognize the clear command to not be anxious. This does not mean that they will suddenly stop being anxious or fearful and never be that way again. It *does* mean that to the degree people can respond positively when anxieties loom large, they will increasingly discover more peace permeating their minds and relationships.

Question 14. This peace of God does not just happen. As with all aspects of the fruit of the Spirit, it comes from our obedience to God's commands and with his enabling.

STUDY 5: PATIENCE

Question 5. To fully understand God's patience, we must understand his righteous wrath. Many people shy away from the biblical teaching of God's wrath because they divorce it from his love and righteousness and imagine that it is tainted with human wrath's unfairness. But this is not possible. God's wrath must always be seen in connection with God's love. The slowness of God's anger is a positive expression of his love for sinners and a practical means of allowing for all manner of rectification of a bad situation. This is divine *makrothumia*—anger properly handled.

STUDY 6: KINDNESS

Question 6. It was common in that day and time for conquering kings to exterminate all family members of the previous ruler in order to prevent a challenge to the throne.

Question 7. The Hebrew word for *kindness* literally means "to bow the head, treat courteously and appropriately." David had known God's kindness and also Jonathan's remarkable affection and friendship. Thus David's kindness was the offspring of the kindness of others. "Mephibosheth was not only permitted life and property, he was given an honoured place at court; in this generosity David went beyond what his covenant with Jonathan had required—it was, in fact, the 'kindness of God' (2 Samuel 9:3)" (*New Bible Commentary,* rev. ed., Grand Rapids: Eerdmans, 1970, p. 306).

Question 11. Grace is God's undeserved favor. Think about how this shows up in his kind actions to us.

Study 7: Goodness

Question 3. We are told in Scripture that because God is good, what he does is good. His act of creation was good (see Genesis 1:31), his laws are good and perfect (see Psalm 19:7), and his goodness is translated to us through his will, which is also good (see Romans 12:2).

Question 5. Scripture focuses on *good* as an eternal reality, a quality described in what God has said and demonstrated in what God has done. The Christian understanding of goodness, radically different from the secular view, finds its reality in God's goodness shown in word, work, and will. Secular society finds goodness in the idea that humans in and of themselves are the standard for good.

Question 6. Paul was talking in this passage about his present experience as a Christian, and the struggle he continued to have against sin.

Question 11. It is all too easy to secretly relish that which is wrong but respectable and to admire that which is evil but acceptable.

Question 12. Clinging to the good is like hanging on to a rope when you're tired. It is working conscientiously when you're bored, sticking with your marriage when you're disappointed, and being committed in your church when it's going nowhere. It is holding on through disappointment, persevering in discouragement, and pressing on through disillusionment.

Question 13. The ongoing battle of good and evil requires both defensive and offensive postures. There are times to be passive and times to be active. Goodness doesn't come naturally; it requires a decision.

Study 8: Faithfulness

Question 5. When we consider faithfulness, our starting point must be God. Faith is built into the fiber of human experience. It is God's way of allowing humanity to experience and exhibit God's faithfulness. We can trust God's love and goodness and faithfulness toward us. This in turn gives us a pushing off point to be faithful in our commitments, in doctrinal purity, and in persecution. We can be reflections of God's faithfulness.

Question 8. It is the Spirit who opens our eyes to Scripture's revelation of God's faithfulness. The Holy Spirit brings to our minds and hearts an understanding of our needs—and our needs can only be met by the benefits of God's faithful love. It is the Holy Spirit who stimulates us to responses of faith, expressions of trust, and exclamations of praise based on God's faithfulness.

Study 9: Meekness

Question 2. "Moses didn't have a Jewish wife because he lived with the Egyptians the first 40 years of his life, and in the desert the next 40 years. The woman is probably not Zipporah, his first wife, who was a Midianite (See Exodus 2:21). A

Cushite was an Ethiopian. There is no explanation given for why Miriam and Aaron objected to this woman" (*Life Application Bible,* p. 233).

Question 4. Moses made no attempt to explain his unique status with God. His gentleness and meekness were most beautifully shown in his reaction to Miriam's leprosy.

Question 7. The Greek word translated "gentle" is *praotes,* meaning "meekness." Jesus exhibited gentleness and meekness in the face of constant criticism from the Pharisees, in his triumphal entry to Jerusalem on a humble donkey, in his betrayal at the Garden of Gethsemane, and in his biased trial. But in Jesus' case, as with Moses and others, he was submissive because he chose to be strong. His actions came from a conscious decision not to be assertive. Meekness is the strength of backing off from a fight you could win and a point you could nail down in order to prevent the damage that would be done and for the sake of the greater issues at stake.

Question 8. Meekness, being part of the nature of Christ, becomes a learning experience for his disciples as they are yoked to him. Not only does the life of Christ model meekness, but commitment to him enables disciples to develop it in their lives. In much the same way that the farmer would lay the heavy wooden yoke over the shoulder of both the old ox and the young one in order that they might walk and work in step, so the Lord teaches meekness one step at a time to those who walk with him.

Study 10: Self-Control

Question 4. The analogy of an athlete would have been especially familiar to Paul's readers in Corinth, since the famous ancient Isthmian Games were held in the environs of their city. Paul urges the self-mastery and total commitment that an athlete must have, but the goals of the Christian are eternity and eternal values.

Question 10. When the struggle against sin or the demands of disciplined living get too heavy, turn again to our living Lord who loves us and will give us grace to keep on going. He struggled in the Garden of Gethsemane but ultimately prayed, "Not my will, but yours be done." Ask for God's Spirit to empower you to make the necessary decisions and adjustments to be able to pray this, too, and to make it stick. That is self-control; that is the Spirit life.

What Should We Study Next?

I f you enjoyed this Fisherman Bible Studyguide, you might want to explore our full line of Fisherman Resources and Bible Studyguides. The following books offer time-tested Fisherman inductive Bible studies for individuals or groups.

FISHERMAN RESOURCES

- *The Art of Spiritual Listening: Responding to God's Voice Amid the Noise of Life* by Alice Fryling
Balm in Gilead by Dudley Delffs
The Essential Bible Guide by Whitney T. Kuniholm
Questions from the God Who Needs No Answers: What Is He Really Asking of You? by Carolyn and Craig Williford
- *Reckless Faith: Living Passionately As Imperfect Christians* by Jo Kadlecek
- *Soul Strength: Spiritual Courage for the Battles of Life* by Pam Lau

FISHERMAN BIBLE STUDYGUIDES

Topical Studies
Angels by Vinita Hampton Wright
Becoming Women of Purpose by Ruth Haley Barton
Building Your House on the Lord: A Firm Foundation for Family Life (Revised Edition) by Steve and Dee Brestin

Discipleship: The Growing Christian's Lifestyle by James and
  Martha Reapsome

*Doing Justice, Showing Mercy: Christian Action in Today's
  World* by Vinita Hampton Wright

Encouraging Others: Biblical Models for Caring by Lin Johnson

The End Times: Discovering What the Bible Says by E. Michael
  Rusten

Examining the Claims of Jesus by Dee Brestin

Friendship: Portraits in God's Family Album by Steve and Dee
  Brestin

The Fruit of the Spirit: Cultivating Christlike Character by
  Stuart Briscoe

Great Doctrines of the Bible by Stephen Board

Great Passages of the Bible by Carol Plueddemann

Great Prayers of the Bible by Carol Plueddemann

➙ *Growing Through Life's Challenges* by James and Martha
  Reapsome

Guidance & God's Will by Tom and Joan Stark

Heart Renewal: Finding Spiritual Refreshment by Ruth Goring

Higher Ground: Steps Toward Christian Maturity by Steve and
  Dee Brestin

➙ *Images of Redemption: God's Unfolding Plan Through the Bible*
  by Ruth E. Van Reken

Integrity: Character from the Inside Out by Ted W. Engstrom
  and Robert C. Larson

Lifestyle Priorities by John White

➙ *Marriage: Learning from Couples in Scripture* by R. Paul and
  Gail Stevens

Miracles by Robbie Castleman

One Body, One Spirit: Building Relationships in the Church by
  Dale and Sandy Larsen

The Parables of Jesus by Gladys Hunt

Parenting with Purpose and Grace: Wisdom for Responding to Your Child's Deepest Needs by Alice Fryling

Prayer: Discovering What Scripture Says by Timothy Jones and Jill Zook-Jones

The Prophets: God's Truth Tellers by Vinita Hampton Wright

Proverbs and Parables: God's Wisdom for Living by Dee Brestin

— *Satisfying Work: Christian Living from Nine to Five* by R. Paul Stevens and Gerry Schoberg

Senior Saints: Growing Older in God's Family by James and Martha Reapsome

The Sermon on the Mount: The God Who Understands Me by Gladys M. Hunt

— *Speaking Wisely: Exploring the Power of Words* by Poppy Smith

Spiritual Disciplines: The Tasks of a Joyful Life by Larry Sibley

Spiritual Gifts by Karen Dockrey

Spiritual Hunger: Filling Your Deepest Longings by Jim and Carol Plueddemann

A Spiritual Legacy: Faith for the Next Generation by Chuck and Winnie Christensen

Spiritual Warfare: Disarming the Enemy Through the Power of God by A. Scott Moreau

The Ten Commandments: God's Rules for Living by Stuart Briscoe

Ultimate Hope for Changing Times by Dale and Sandy Larsen

When Faith Is All You Have: A Study of Hebrews 11 by Ruth E. Van Reken

Where Your Treasure Is: What the Bible Says About Money by James and Martha Reapsome

Who Is God? by David P. Seemuth

Who Is Jesus? In His Own Words by Ruth E. Van Reken

Who Is the Holy Spirit? by Barbara H. Knuckles and Ruth E.
     Van Reken
Wisdom for Today's Woman: Insights from Esther by Poppy
     Smith
Witnesses to All the World: God's Heart for the Nations by Jim
     and Carol Plueddemann
Women at Midlife: Embracing the Challenges by Jeanie Miley
Worship: Discovering What Scripture Says by Larry Sibley

Bible Book Studies
Genesis: Walking with God by Margaret Fromer and Sharrel
     Keyes
Exodus: God Our Deliverer by Dale and Sandy Larsen
Ruth: Relationships That Bring Life by Ruth Haley Barton
Ezra and Nehemiah: A Time to Rebuild by James Reapsome
(For Esther, see Topical Studies, *Wisdom for Today's Woman*)
— *Job: Trusting Through Trials* by Ron Klug
Psalms: A Guide to Prayer and Praise by Ron Klug
Proverbs: Wisdom That Works by Vinita Hampton Wright
Ecclesiastes: A Time for Everything by Stephen Board
Song of Songs: A Dialogue of Intimacy by James Reapsome
Jeremiah: The Man and His Message by James Reapsome
Jonah, Habakkuk, and Malachi: Living Responsibly by
     Margaret Fromer and Sharrel Keyes
Matthew: People of the Kingdom by Larry Sibley
Mark: God in Action by Chuck and Winnie Christensen
Luke: Following Jesus by Sharrel Keyes
John: An Eyewitness Account of the Son of God by Whitney T.
     Kuniholm
Acts 1–12: God Moves in the Early Church by Chuck and
     Winnie Christensen

Acts 13–28, see *Paul* under Character Studies

Romans: The Christian Story by James Reapsome

1 Corinthians: Problems and Solutions in a Growing Church by Charles and Ann Hummel

Strengthened to Serve: 2 Corinthians by Jim and Carol Plueddemann

Galatians, Titus, and Philemon: Freedom in Christ by Whitney Kuniholm

Ephesians: Living in God's Household by Robert Baylis

Philippians: God's Guide to Joy by Ron Klug

Colossians: Focus on Christ by Luci Shaw

Letters to the Thessalonians by Margaret Fromer and Sharrel Keyes

Letters to Timothy: Discipleship in Action by Margaret Fromer and Sharrel Keyes

Hebrews: Foundations for Faith by Gladys Hunt

James: Faith in Action by Chuck and Winnie Christensen

1 and 2 Peter, Jude: Called for a Purpose by Steve and Dee Brestin

1, 2, 3 John: How Should a Christian Live? by Dee Brestin

Revelation: The Lamb Who Is the Lion by Gladys Hunt

Bible Character Studies

Abraham: Model of Faith by James Reapsome

David: Man After God's Own Heart by Robbie Castleman

Elijah: Obedience in a Threatening World by Robbie Castleman

Great People of the Bible by Carol Plueddemann

King David: Trusting God for a Lifetime by Robbie Castleman

Men Like Us: Ordinary Men, Extraordinary God by Paul Heidebrecht and Ted Scheuermann

Moses: Encountering God by Greg Asimakoupoulos

Paul: Thirteenth Apostle (Acts 13–28) by Chuck and Winnie
   Christensen

Women Like Us: Wisdom for Today's Issues by Ruth Haley
   Barton

Women Who Achieved for God by Winnie Christensen

Women Who Believed God by Winnie Christensen